52-Week Mental Health Journal

52-Week Mental Health Journal

GUIDED PROMPTS AND SELF-REFLECTION
TO REDUCE STRESS AND IMPROVE WELL-BEING

Cynthia Catchings, LCSW-S, LCSW-C, MSSW

Published by Callisto Publishing LLC C/O Sourcebooks LLC
P.O. Box 4410, Naperville, Illinois 60567-4410
(630) 961-3900
callistopublishing.com

Printed and bound in China.
WKT 21

This journal belongs to

....

*If you own
this story
you get to write
the ending.*

—BRENÉ BROWN

Introduction

Welcome to this new chapter of your life! I am stoked to share this journal with you, where we will have the opportunity to walk together while you create the life of your dreams. I am a psychotherapist, licensed clinical social worker, certified family trauma professional, and certified mental health integrative medicine professional who has helped hundreds of clients change their lives and reach their goals. For the past 12 years, I have assisted individuals in finding their purpose through therapy and social services. I have traveled to more than 30 countries to learn how people deal with emotional issues and find solutions to their problems. This has allowed me to gather and share great information to help others. Most of that information is included here, and it has changed many of my patients' lives. I know it will make a difference in yours as well.

Making a change in life may feel daunting. Our mental health influences how we think, feel, and behave. If our mental or emotional health is not in shape, making a change may feel even more frightening. It can also affect our ability to cope with stress, overcome daily life obstacles, build relationships, and recover from life's setbacks and challenges. Although mental health issues are different from mental illness, poor mental health can cause mental illness. When this happens, we may start experiencing more severe issues, like depression and anxiety.

Journaling can be an effective tool to help us improve our mental health. This journal can help you keep your thoughts organized, release stress, reflect on those things that affect you or things you are grateful for, achieve your goals, and enhance your sense of well-being and self-esteem. Through writing, reflection, and practice, this journal will help you tackle four core areas that are pillars of good mental and emotional health: calm and resiliency, connection and engagement, healthy living, and goals and purpose. As you start and continue journaling, you will likely notice that you are more focused and mindful and that your life is improving in different areas.

Journaling is a simple but very powerful tool. During the next 52 weeks, which you can begin on any day you choose, you will enjoy the benefits of journaling, which include improving your memory and boosting your mood. Keep your journal where you can see it frequently, such as on your nightstand, and write in it privately. Set a time to write daily and have an alternative option in case something comes up. For example, you can opt to write before going to bed. If that is not possible one night, your alternative time can be in the morning before you get out of bed or when you have a 10-minute break. Write in a place where you are preferably alone and free from interruptions. Give yourself at least five minutes to reflect on what you wrote. Do not feel obligated to write more or less; just write every day. This is your moment to share with yourself, let go, and be yourself. By doing this, you will move forward in this journey you are starting today.

Remember, you can use your journal at any time. I will be beside you as you experience the transformational improvement of your emotional health and overall well-being during this process of inner growth.

Boost Your Mental Health

Congratulations on starting a new chapter in your life that will lead you to happier days. This journal will be your guide and companion while you set about creating the life of your dreams. It will help boost your well-being and improve your mental and emotional health by targeting the weekly journal prompts to the following core areas.

CALM AND RESILIENCY

Resilience gives us the emotional strength to deal with our daily stressors. It does not make our problems disappear, but it helps us deal with them calmly. Being calm also helps us be more resilient. Calmly and effectively managing stress while building resiliency helps us decrease feelings of anxiety and depression, allowing us to live a happier and healthier life. The journal prompts in this area can help you explore a balanced lifestyle in which you have enough time for personal and professional achievements, healthy relationships, and fun.

CONNECTION AND ENGAGEMENT

Humans are social creatures who thrive in communities where interaction and support are present. Belonging to a community, having a sense of purpose, and enjoying healthy relationships support us in life and give our lives meaning, which benefit our emotional health. Studies show the risks of loneliness and social isolation on our mental health and the importance of human connections. The journal prompts in this category are designed to help you stay connected with those close to you to reduce stress, anxiety, and depression, and increase your self-esteem and self-worth.

HEALTHY LIVING

Taking care of our physical health can improve our mental and emotional well-being. By creating simple lifestyle changes, such as following a healthy diet, exercising, or sleeping better, we can feel better, and we will experience fewer aches and pains. Similarly, by taking care of our minds by exercising our brains with new information, such as learning a language or reframing (thinking positively), we can experience fewer depressive symptoms and decrease stress levels. The journal prompts in this category are intended to get you thinking about the changes you want to make and how to go about making them.

GOALS AND PURPOSE

Setting goals and having a sense of purpose can add depth to our lives. Depression and anxiety are two of the main mental health conditions that prevent us from setting goals and finding our purpose, and they sometimes require medical intervention. They typically cause lack of motivation and focus, general overwhelm, and deep sadness or constant fear that prevent us from seeing beyond our unwanted feelings. Through journaling, you can reduce the negative thoughts and feelings that often accompany depression, anxiety, and stress. As a result, you will feel better physically, mentally, and emotionally.

After the 52 weeks of journaling practice, you should experience an improvement in your mood, increased energy, higher motivation, and the ability to reach more goals. Journaling is a personal practice that allows your authentic self to communicate. Just give it a few minutes a day and see all the benefits it brings. I wish you the best on your journaling path. Happy journaling!

* This journal is meant to help you maintain your mental health over the course of a year. If you are in a crisis, or if you simply need someone to talk to, you should find a licensed therapist or counselor either locally or via telehealth.

Calm and Resiliency

1. If you found a magic lamp, what three wishes would you ask for? If all your wishes were granted the next morning, how would you feel?

....

....

....

....

....

2. Reflecting on the wishes you asked for yesterday, which ones are within your control to achieve? Can you make any of them a reality?

....

....

....

....

....

3. List three activities that make you feel happy. How often do you engage in those activities?

....

....

....

....

....

4. What are some of your strengths, and how do you plan to use them to benefit your life moving forward?

....

....

....

....

....

When two friends, like you and me, are in the mood to chat, we have to go about it in a gentler and more dialectical way. By "more dialectical," I mean not only that we give real responses, but that we base our responses solely on what the interlocutor admits that he himself knows. —PLATO

5. Write down a positive phrase to repeat to yourself to help you remain calm when faced with stressful situations. How can it support you?

....

....

....

....

....

6. What might help you become better able to bounce back after setbacks this year?

....

....

....

....

....

7. What do you do to rest or take care of yourself at the end of the week?

....

....

....

....

....

Connection and Engagement

1. How do you stay connected with friends and family throughout the week?

....

....

....

....

....

2. Write yourself a letter, speaking to yourself the way a loving friend or relative would speak to you.

....

....

....

....

....

3. List three people you enjoy talking to. What makes you feel good about talking to each one?

....

....

....

....

....

4. Think about someone you miss but have not talked to
   in a while. What is preventing you from reaching out?
   How could you reach out without feeling uncomfortable?

....

....

....

....

....

5. When was the last time you had fun with a friend?
   What did you do that day? What aspects of your time
   with that person made you feel good?

....

....

....

....

....

6. Draft notes to two of your friends letting them know why you are grateful for their friendship. Copy them over to stationery and mail them.

....

....

....

....

....

7. List an activity you can do with people you like each day for the next seven days.

....

....

....

....

....

Healthy Living

1. What are some of the lifestyle changes you would like to make in your life?

....

....

....

....

....

2. Reflecting on what you wrote about yesterday, how can you implement those changes, and what do you need to start the process?

....

....

....

....

....

3. Describe the best way to take care of your body. What are you doing to accomplish it?

....

....

....

....

....

4. What causes stress in your life? What steps have you
taken to reduce or alleviate the cause?

....

....

....

....

....

5. Reflect on a situation you experienced when your stress
level was very high. What were some of the physical and
emotional symptoms you were feeling?

....

....

....

....

....

6. Describe two things you normally do to reduce stress. How do you feel after you do them?

....

....

....

....

....

7. Sit comfortably. For a minute or two, mentally scan your body from your toes to your head and back again, briefly noting any sensations. How did you feel during and after the activity?

....

....

....

....

....

Goals and Purpose

1. What goals do you hope to accomplish by using this 52-week journal?

....

....

....

....

....

2. Describe how you can accomplish the goals you identified yesterday.

....

....

....

....

....

3. When you were little, you dreamed of what you would be when you grew up. Did you achieve your dream? How? If not, what prevented you from pursuing it?

....

....

....

....

....

4. What stops you from reaching your goals? What motivates
you to reach them?

....

....

....

....

....

5. If you had the opportunity to start a new job anywhere,
where would you like to work and what do you see
yourself doing?

....

....

....

....

....

6. If you had a time machine, would you travel to the past
or the future? What would be your purpose for going
to that time? What goals would you set for your trip?

....

....

....

....

....

7. Looking forward to next week, what can you do to stay better organized and accomplish your objectives?

....

....

....

....

....

Calm and Resiliency

1. Write down what worries you. Allow yourself to leave it here. Once you feel calmer, come back to this page and read what you wrote.

....

....

....

....

....

2. Think of a positive word, like "peace" or "happiness." Throughout the day, focus on that word and notice things that make you feel that way. What might you notice?

....

....

....

....

....

What is done in love is done well.

—VINCENT VAN GOGH

3. You can reduce stress and anxiety by breathing. Try it: Inhale to a count of four, hold to a count of seven, and exhale to a count of eight. Repeat. Afterward, jot down how you feel.

....

....

....

....

....

4. What are three physical traits and three nonphysical traits that make you feel good about yourself?

....

....

....

....

....

5. Share a story about a time when you overcame a difficult situation. How did you feel afterward?

....

....

....

....

....

6. Building connections with others increases our resilience. What can you do today to connect with someone or to be more social?

....

....

....

....

....

7. Self-care includes giving yourself a chance to unwind and relax. What steps can you take to create a peaceful space at home where you can feel calm and recharge?

....

....

....

....

....

Connection and Engagement

1. What activity with others keeps you completely engaged and feeling happy after you have done it? Describe why it brings you so much happiness.

....

....

....

....

....

2. Think about a moment when you felt fully connected to someone. Describe the situation and the feelings you experienced.

....

....

....

....

....

3. Take a moment to think about people you love but have not seen in a while. What are some ways you could reconnect with them? Come up with an idea for each person.

....

....

....

....

....

4. Write about a situation when you felt as if you had no choice but to go to a place or event and ended up meeting someone there who became important in your life.

....

....

....

....

....

5. What is the best compliment you remember receiving from another person? Why did it make you feel good?

....

....

....

....

....

6. Share three of your favorite memories of times spent with friends or loved ones. Why are these memories special to you?

....

....

....

....

....

7. Think about someone—it could be anyone—you would like to send a note to. Draft the letter here and then copy it over to a card or stationery and mail it.

....

....

....

....

....

Healthy Living

1. List the activities you do to take care of yourself. Place a check mark next to each one that you do at least three times a week.

....

....

....

....

....

2. Having a designated "fun time" place or corner at home can help improve your mood. How can you make this space special to you?

....

....

....

....

....

3. Share five ways to help you prioritize your physical and emotional well-being. What do you need to make them happen and when can you start practicing them?

....

....

....

....

....

4. Forming habits of happiness requires effort and practice. What habits can you start practicing today to help you feel happier?

....

....

....

....

....

5. Think about a time when you were overly worried but everything resolved satisfactorily. What would you do differently in the same situation to avoid excessive worry?

....

....

....

....

....

6. List 5 to 10 things you would like to do or change to more fully enjoy your living space. Then number them in the order you'd like to accomplish them.

....

....

....

....

....

....

....

....

....

7. Look at yesterday's prompt. What can you do today to start, continue, or finish each of those changes or activities? What is your motivation to do it?

....

....

....

....

....

Goals and Purpose

1. Think about all your accomplishments. What goal would you still like to accomplish? Describe what has prevented you from reaching it.

....

....

....

....

....

2. Look back at yesterday's prompt. Create a timeline and break down your goal into small tasks you can complete weekly until you reach your goal.

....

....

....

....

....

3. Is there a professional dream you would like to pursue? Describe the first step you can take to make it a reality.

....

....

....

....

....

4. If you could visit another town or state this weekend, where would you go and what would you do there?

....

....

....

....

....

5. Write a letter to the person you will be three years in the future, congratulating yourself on all your accomplishments. Specify your accomplishments.

....

....

....

....

....

6. List four activities that bring you happiness that you have not participated in lately. Create a plan to do them one at a time over the next four weekends.

....

....

....

....

....

7. What can you do to improve your time management and focus in the upcoming week?

....

....

....

....

....

Calm and Resiliency

1. What does a perfect morning look like to you? What steps can you take to have that type of morning every day?

....

....

....

....

....

2. List five of your favorite songs. How does each song make you feel?

....

....

....

....

....

It is in our power to be virtuous or vicious.

—ARISTOTLE

3. Think about the last time you felt anxious or sad. What did you learn from the experience once the anxiety or sadness went away?

....

....

....

....

....

4. Think of an activity that brings you a sense of peace and well-being. What does it look like? How does it feel?

....

....

....

....

....

5. What is your favorite color? Close your eyes and imagine various items in that color for a moment. Open your eyes and share how you feel.

....

....

....

....

....

6. Imagine watching a sunrise from a beautiful setting, such as on a beach, mountain, or terrace. What sounds do you hear and what physical sensations do you feel?

....

....

....

....

....

7. What tools do you use to move forward despite negative events—for example, thinking positively or exercising? Describe your techniques and discuss other useful strategies.

....

....

....

....

....

Connection and Engagement

1. If you could organize the perfect reunion with people you love, who would you invite to the gathering and what activities would you plan for the event?

....

....

....

....

....

2. Who is your best friend? What qualities about them make you feel uplifted?

....

....

....

....

....

3. List the top 10 people who have positively influenced you and, next to their names, describe their impact.

....

....

....

....

....

....

....

....

....

....

4. What are some ways you can be kind to others today or tomorrow? How would being kind to them make you feel?

....

....

....

....

....

5. What is on your bucket list that you can do with another person? Who would you ask to tag along with you for the most fun?

....

....

....

....

....

6. If you won the lottery, who would you choose to help? What would you do for that group or person?

....

....

....

....

....

7. What are some tasks you can do next week to support your coworkers, friends, or family members? How would supporting them make you feel?

....

....

....

....

....

Healthy Living

1. List your three favorite healthy foods. How often do you eat them?

....

....

....

....

....

2. On a scale of 1 to 10, how healthy would you rate your daily habits? What changes do you need to make to rate them higher?

....

....

....

....

....

3. How do you reward yourself at the end of the day? Is that working for you?

....

....

....

....

....

4. Close your eyes for one minute and visualize your favorite
place. Describe how that place makes you feel.

....

....

....

....

....

5. What time of the day do you feel your best? What do you
normally do during those hours?

....

....

....

....

....

6. What are your favorite healthy beverages? How can you
enjoy them more often during your day?

....

....

....

....

....

7. When you experience stress, what are three positive actions you take to feel better?

....

....

....

....

....

Goals and Purpose

1. List your needs and goals for the week ahead. How can you prioritize your needs so that you can meet your goals?

....

....

....

....

....

2. What has been motivating you to reach your goals lately?

....

....

....

....

....

3. How do you feel when you do not meet your goals?

....

....

....

....

....

4. What thoughts limit you or prevent you from reaching your goals?

....

....

....

....

....

5. What positive thoughts and actions can you use to reduce or eliminate the negative thoughts you listed yesterday?

....

....

....

....

....

6. What three things inspire you to keep going every day?

....

....

....

....

....

7. What does success mean to you? Describe how it looks.

....

....

....

....

....

Calm and Resiliency

1. Think of a song that makes you feel calm. What is the song about?

....

....

....

....

....

2. List seven things that can help you bounce back after a setback.

....

....

....

....

....

Don't be afraid of perfection.
You'll never attain it!

—SALVADOR DALÍ

3. Write down three phrases you need to hear from a friend or loved one to feel better. How can those words help you today? Say them to yourself.

....

....

....

....

....

4. Share a story about a time when you felt strong and resilient during and after a difficult situation.

....

....

....

....

....

5. What type of weather makes you feel good? What do you enjoy doing outdoors in that type of weather?

....

....

....

....

....

6. Describe one of your favorite childhood memories.

....

....

....

....

....

7. Look around the room. Pick out an item that brings up a good memory. Describe the memory.

....

....

....

....

....

Connection and Engagement

1. What do you like to do when you spend time with your friends?

....

....

....

....

....

2. Describe your favorite memory of time spent with a loved one last year.

....

....

....

....

....

3. List three things you admire about a specific friend or family member. Why do you admire those qualities?

....

....

....

....

....

4. Who is the first person you usually contact when you need help? What kind of help has that person given you?

....

....

....

....

....

5. What is the best advice a friend or relative has given you? Did you take it? What was the outcome?

....

....

....

....

....

6. How do you think your closest friend would describe you physically, mentally, and emotionally?

....

....

....

....

....

7. Who was kind to you this week, and what can you do to reciprocate?

....

....

....

....

....

Healthy Living

1. Taking time to stretch or breathe deeply throughout the day can help keep you alert and limber. List five physical activities you can practice two to three times a day at home or work.

....

....

....

....

....

2. Observe your posture and straighten your back. Take a deep breath. How does that make you feel?

....

....

....

....

....

3. When was the last time you drank eight glasses of water in a day? What steps can you take to meet this goal every day?

....

....

....

....

....

4. Describe how you have been sleeping the last three
nights. Is there something you need to change to get
a better night's sleep?

....

....

....

....

....

5. A nightly routine can improve your sleep. Create a nightly
routine that can help you feel more rested in the morning.

....

....

....

....

....

6. Describe a dream you had that caused you to wake up feeling happy or energetic.

....

....

....

....

....

7. Do you prefer to drink water, tea, juice, or coffee? Why is that your preference, and how do you feel after drinking that beverage?

....

....

....

....

....

Goals and Purpose

1. What goal would you like to set for yourself this week? It could be as simple as going to bed earlier or drinking more water. How would it benefit you?

....

....

....

....

....

2. You enjoy doing specific things that make you or others happy. Those things create purpose. What is your life purpose as of today?

....

....

....

....

....

3. If you could create the perfect space at home to plan and organize your days, how would it look?

....

....

....

....

....

4. Imagine that you won the lottery. How would your life be different in terms of being able to fulfill your life purpose? How would it be the same?

....

....

....

....

....

5. If a genie granted you one wish, what would you wish for in order to have a happier life? How would getting that make you happier?

....

....

....

....

....

6. What are your top three goals for the rest of this week? How can you accomplish them?

....

....

....

....

....

7. What three things do you enjoy the most about your job or hobby? Why are those tasks or qualities enjoyable?

....

....

....

....

....

Calm and Resiliency

1. Close your eyes, take a deep breath, and think about a specific age. Recall the first memory that pops into your mind about that age. Write about it.

....

....

....

....

....

2. If you could be either at the beach or in the mountains this weekend, which would you choose and why?

....

....

....

....

....

New and different waters flow around
those who step into the same river.

—HERACLITUS

3. Imagine that you had the power to change the past. What would you change? In what way do you think your present would be different?

....

....

....

....

....

4. Which type of weather makes you feel calm: sunshine or rain showers? Describe the feeling of calmness you have on that kind of day.

....

....

....

....

....

5. List the top 10 songs that make you feel good about yourself.

....

....

....

....

....

....

....

....

....

....

6. What is going well in your life today? How does that make you feel?

....

....

....

....

....

7. List five enjoyable things you can do next week. Take some time to schedule them in.

....

....

....

....

....

Connection and Engagement

1. Who are the people in your life who make you feel happy and alive? Share what they do to make you feel this way.

....

....

....

....

....

2. If you could throw a party for your closest friend, what theme would you choose and why?

....

....

....

....

....

3. You just won a trip for two to your favorite country! Who would you invite and why?

....

....

....

....

....

4. What type of conversation makes you feel more connected to the people you spend time with?

....

....

....

....

....

5. Describe two of your favorite places in your city or town where people congregate.

....

....

....

....

....

6. Who would you like to see in concert? What about being at the concert would make you feel happy?

....

....

....

....

....

7. List five positive words that describe your closest friend or family member. Reflect on those qualities and identify what you like about them.

....

....

....

....

....

Healthy Living

1. Step outside or look through a window, and gaze up at the sky for a few minutes. Describe what you saw and how you felt.

....

....

....

....

....

2. How do you see yourself right now? How does that compare to how you would like to see yourself?

....

....

....

....

....

3. If you were a professional athlete, what sport would you play? What healthy habits would you need in your life to play that sport?

....

....

....

....

....

4. Think about the last time you went for a walk, hike, or run. Describe how you felt.

....

....

....

....

....

5. Share your thoughts about nutrition and exercise.

....

....

....

....

....

6. What emotions do you experience when you think about food? Are these feelings you want to change?

....

....

....

....

....

7. If you spent a day being completely healthy, whatever that means to you, what would that look like from beginning to end?

....

....

....

....

....

Goals and Purpose

1. Have you done anything lately to help make your friends or family members feel good? Why or why not?

....

....

....

....

....

2. What are 10 meaningful things you can do for others to help make them happy?

....

....

....

....

....

3. When you are gone, what would you like to be remembered for?

....

....

....

....

....

4. If you could choose between wealth or perfect health, which would you choose and why?

....

....

....

....

....

5. What are three tasks or activities you can do to feel accomplished this week?

....

....

....

....

....

6. What has been one of your greatest accomplishments? Why do you consider it among the greatest?

....

....

....

....

....

7. If you could go to a museum with a friend or family member this weekend, what type of museum would you visit and who would you go with?

....

....

....

....

....

Calm and Resiliency

1. List five things, sounds, or activities that calm you down when you feel upset. How can you be more mindful and use them in the future?

....

....

....

....

....

2. If you couldn't use your phone for 24 hours, what other activities would you concentrate on?

....

....

....

....

....

Every child is an artist. The problem is how to remain an artist once he grows up.

—**PABLO PICASSO**

3. Set a timer for three minutes and sit quietly. When the timer goes off, write down what you thought about.

....

....

....

....

....

4. What activity helps boost your mood? Describe how you feel after you do it.

....

....

....

....

....

5. Imagine that you are sitting by a large body of water. Jot down what you see, hear, smell, and feel.

....

....

....

....

....

6. Complete this sentence: "Today I feel good about myself because . . ."

....

....

....

....

....

7. Think of a time when you felt afraid but kept going despite your fear. Describe it.

....

....

....

....

....

Connection and Engagement

1. What are some things you enjoy doing with coworkers, classmates, or acquaintances?

....

....

....

....

....

2. In what ways would you like to become involved in your community?

....

....

....

....

....

3. Imagine walking along the shore with one of your closest friends. What subjects would you discuss?

....

....

....

....

....

4. Who was your first best friend? What do you remember
doing together?

....

....

....

....

....

5. Think about the last movie you saw in a movie theater.
What did you like about the experience of being in the
theater?

....

....

....

....

....

6. Share a happy story about a time when you were in elementary school.

....

....

....

....

....

7. If you could travel to a fantasy land, who would you take with you and what would you do there?

....

....

....

....

....

Healthy Living

1. What new language would you like to learn? Why that one? Where would you go to practice it?

....

....

....

....

....

2. What TV show makes you feel good? Share what you like about it and describe how it makes you feel.

....

....

....

....

....

3. If you won a free cruise to any destination, where would you go? What activities would you do during the trip that would make you feel happy and energized?

....

....

....

....

....

4. Think about a time when you felt you were living a healthy life. What were you doing to take care of yourself?

....

....

....

....

....

5. Describe three of your favorite outfits. How do you feel when you wear each one?

....

....

....

....

....

6. What do you usually take pictures of and why? If someone gifted you a high-quality camera, would you take different types of photos, and if so, what would you capture?

....

....

....

....

....

7. How do you take care of yourself after a busy week?

....

....

....

....

....

Goals and Purpose

1. Write a note to yourself five years from now discussing three five-year goals you have accomplished.

....

....

....

....

....

2. Describe the feelings that come up when you think about your greatest accomplishment.

....

....

....

....

....

3. What are you grateful for today?

....

....

....

....

....

4. If you could go to another planet and breathe the atmosphere, what would you do there and what would you see?

....

....

....

....

....

5. If money were no object, what would you devote your life to? Who would benefit?

....

....

....

....

....

6. Draft a thank-you note to your most impactful high school teacher. If you can still contact them, copy it over to stationery and mail it.

....

....

....

....

....

7. If you could move to another location for your dream job, what would it be and where would you live?

....

....

....

....

....

Calm and Resiliency

1. List five of your usual coping mechanisms for facing difficulties.

....

....

....

....

....

2. Describe how it feels to face something that scares you.

....

....

....

....

....

What makes the desert so beautiful
is that it hides a well, somewhere.

—ANTOINE DE SAINT-EXUPÉRY

3. When you feel scared or overwhelmed by a situation, how can you reassure yourself that you can move forward?

....

....

....

....

....

4. What types of situations and/or encounters cause you to feel irritated? Describe the types of thoughts you have in those circumstances.

....

....

....

....

....

5. Think about a particularly difficult day and the feelings you were having. What eventually made you feel better?

....

....

....

....

....

6. List five activities that help you feel calm when you do them. How long does the sense of calm last?

....

....

....

....

....

7. When things do not go the way you hoped or expected they would, describe the thoughts and feelings you usually have.

....

....

....

....

....

Connection and Engagement

1. What is the kindest thing someone has done for you? Why do you still remember it?

....

....

....

....

....

2. Write about the last time someone made you laugh.

....

....

....

....

....

3. Describe a perfect day with a friend or family member.

....

....

....

....

....

4. Draft a thank-you note to the last person who did something good for you. Copy it over to stationery and mail it.

....

....

....

....

....

5. List five questions you can ask the next time you meet someone new.

....

....

....

....

....

6. If you could hang out with one of your old friends, who would you be with and where would you go? What would you talk about?

....

....

....

....

....

7. Describe the perfect date with your significant other or someone you have yet to meet.

....

....

....

....

....

Healthy Living

1. Mentally, emotionally, and physically, how do you feel today? Rate each on a scale from 1 to 10. How can you increase your rating, if needed?

....

....

....

....

....

2. Do you enjoy spending time in the sun or do you prefer cloudy days? Why?

....

....

....

....

....

3. List the foods that make you feel good or energized when you eat them.

....

....

....

....

....

4. Think about what you would consider a perfect bedroom
to rest and relax in. Describe it.

....

....

....

....

....

5. If you could have a tennis court, an Olympic-size swimming
pool, or a fully equipped gym in your house, which would
you choose and why?

....

....

....

....

....

6. If you were not afraid, what three activities would you try?

....

....

....

....

....

7. Describe how you feel when you have a good week.

....

....

....

....

....

Goals and Purpose

1. What motivates you when trying to reach a personal goal? Why do you find that motivating?

....

....

....

....

....

2. Describe the steps you take to feel better when you are faced with something that scares you or makes you feel anxious.

....

....

....

....

....

3. If you could find a cure for either depression or anxiety, which issue would you focus your efforts on? Why?

....

....

....

....

....

4. List three goals you have accomplished in the past.
What helped or motivated you to reach them?

....

....

....

....

....

5. If you could achieve one goal in your lifetime, what would
it be?

....

....

....

....

....

6. What is holding you back from reaching the goal you
wrote about yesterday?

....

....

....

....

....

7. If a friend told you that they were afraid to take a risk, what would you say to encourage them to go for it?

....

....

....

....

....

Calm and Resiliency

1. Considering everything you have watched over the years, what is your all-time favorite TV show? What about it makes it your favorite?

....

....

....

....

....

2. Think of a particular situation that makes you feel anxious. How do you calm yourself when you find yourself in that type of situation?

....

....

....

....

....

You can't use up creativity.
The more you use, the more you have.

—MAYA ANGELOU

3. List three things that stressed you out this week. What can you do to cope better if those things happen again?

....

....

....

....

....

4. Looking back at yesterday's prompt, write a letter to your stress sharing how you are now in control and feeling better.

....

....

....

....

....

5. What stands out as the most upsetting event that occurred within the last two weeks? What did you do to bounce back?

....

....

....

....

....

6. If you could remodel your workspace to feel calmer and more productive, describe how it would look.

....

....

....

....

....

7. What three songs give you a sense of empowerment? Describe the qualities associated with that feeling.

....

....

....

....

....

Connection and Engagement

1. List five things you believe your closest friend likes. Share your list with your friend to see if they agree with your choices.

....

....

....

....

....

2. If you had a gift card to buy anything at any store for someone else, what store would you go to and what would you buy?

....

....

....

....

....

3. If you were stranded at an airport for 24 hours, what famous person would you like to find yourself with? Narrate the conversation.

....

....

....

....

....

4. Share five things your support system does for you that make you feel cared for.

....

....

....

....

....

5. List three things you would like to do this weekend with someone you love.

....

....

....

....

....

6. Draft an apology letter to someone you hurt in the past.
If you want to share it with them, copy it to a piece of
stationery and mail it.

....

....

....

....

....

7. Describe the perfect day spending time with people in
your community.

....

....

....

....

....

Healthy Living

1. List three to five things you can do when you feel anxious or depressed to feel better mentally.

....

....

....

....

....

2. Describe the elements of a perfect lunch, including the setting, the dishes, and the food and beverages served.

....

....

....

....

....

3. What do you do to ensure that you have at least one good meal every day? Do you need to make any changes?

....

....

....

....

....

4. How do you sleep at night? List five things you can do to improve the quality of your sleep.

....

....

....

....

....

5. What five physical activities would you like to practice regularly to improve your health and have fun?

....

....

....

....

....

6. Write a short story about a superhero who can do everything you would like to be able to do.

....

....

....

....

....

7. What steps can you take to become the superhero you wrote about yesterday?

....

....

....

....

....

Goals and Purpose

1. What is going right in your life today?

....

....

....

....

....

2. Write two statements about things that are going wrong in your life. Now, flip these statements around to make them positive.

....

....

....

....

....

3. Draw a picture of a person, place, or thing that makes you happy. Describe how you feel when you look at what you've drawn.

....

....

....

....

....

4. Being mindful means being present, interested, and proactive. Write a list of strategies for how you can be more mindful about reaching your goals.

....

....

....

....

....

5. Describe what a perfect day looks like to you. How can you be more purposeful about making tomorrow closer to what you just described?

....

....

....

....

....

6. List three of your self-improvement goals. What steps can you take to achieve them?

....

....

....

....

....

7. What do you do to make the moments in your life more memorable?

....

....

....

....

....

Calm and Resiliency

1. Describe three places in your town or city that give you a sense of peace when you visit them.

....

....

....

....

....

2. In what part of your home do you generally feel the calmest? What activities could you do in that area to make it even more relaxing?

....

....

....

....

....

To know is nothing at all;
to imagine is everything.

—ANATOLE FRANCE

3. Write about one of your most treasured items in your home. Why do you treasure it?

....

....

....

....

....

4. Take a deep breath or two, and then write about what brings you a sense of peace.

....

....

....

....

....

5. How would your friends describe you when you are in a happy mood?

....

....

....

....

....

6. Think about your clothes. What colors do you wear most
often? Which colors make you feel peaceful? Which make
you feel strong?

....

....

....

....

....

7. Think about the last time you cried. Once all the tears
were spent, how did you feel?

....

....

....

....

....

Connection and Engagement

1. Who are your two closest friends? Describe their personalities and how they each make you feel.

....

....

....

....

....

2. When you feel sad, who do you usually call? What does that person say or do to help you feel better?

....

....

....

....

....

3. If you feel sad or anxious, what types of group or partner activities can you do to help you feel better?

....

....

....

....

....

4. What are three things you would like to experience with a friend this month?

....

....

....

....

....

5. Think about a milestone you would like to accomplish with the help of someone you admire. How could you make it a reality?

....

....

....

....

....

6. Name five people you are close to. What can you do, create, or get for them to make them feel appreciated?

....

....

....

....

....

7. Think about a friend you have not been in touch with recently. Draft a note checking in with them and copy it over to an e-mail or text—or send a letter.

....

....

....

....

....

Healthy Living

1. On a scale of 1 to 10, how would you rate your sleeping habits? If you rated lower than a 10, what is in the way?

....

....

....

....

....

2. If you could eliminate one of your school assignments or job responsibilities today, which would it be? Why?

....

....

....

....

....

3. How do you feel on a windy day, a rainy day, a sunny day, and a chilly day? Describe the feelings.

....

....

....

....

....

4. What activity or hobby would you like to start practicing? What do you think you will like about it?

....

....

....

....

....

5. Is there something worrying you this week? What steps can you take to resolve the worry?

....

....

....

....

....

6. What day of the week do you enjoy the most? What do you typically do that day?

....

....

....

....

....

7. What is your favorite activity to do on a day like today? Why?

....

....

....

....

....

Goals and Purpose

1. What short-term goal would you like to accomplish this week?

....

....

....

....

....

2. Write down your favorite affirmation or positive thought. How often do you use it? If not often, how can you start using it more?

....

....

....

....

....

3. Is there something you wish you had more control over? If you had that control, how would things be different?

....

....

....

....

....

4. If you could have lunch with any world leader, who would you choose? What would you talk about?

....

....

....

....

....

5. What changes would you like to see in your community? Is this something you can devote some effort to?

....

....

....

....

....

6. What are some goals you can set for deepening your current relationships?

....

....

....

....

....

7. Thinking about tomorrow, what activities, plans, or things make you feel motivated? Why?

....

....

....

....

....

Calm and Resiliency

1. We may worry when we think too much about the future. What are some ways you can be more mindful of the present moment?

....

....

....

....

....

2. Thinking about things that cause you stress and anxiety, what ideas come to mind to help you reduce them?

....

....

....

....

....

There are always flowers
for those who want to see them.

—HENRI MATISSE

3. Have you ever experienced deep fear or a panic attack? How did you work through it to feel better?

....

....

....

....

....

4. Think about an experience that taught you to be stronger. Share the details.

....

....

....

....

....

5. Describe an outfit in your closet makes you feel comfortable and secure. How often do you wear it?

....

....

....

....

....

6. Helping others feel at ease can help us have better days. What can you do for the people around you to help them experience a sense of calmness?

....

....

....

....

....

7. Reflect on the day-to-day events that made you feel good this week. Which one in particular would you like to relive?

....

....

....

....

....

Connection and Engagement

1. Is there anyone you feel close to that you have not spent time with in more than a month? What will you say to them the next time you see them and what will you do?

....

....

....

....

....

2. Does a particular friend or family member make you feel safe? Who are they and what about them makes you feel secure?

....

....

....

....

....

3. Think about the last conversation you had with your best friend. What was it about?

....

....

....

....

....

4. Do you prefer spending time with funny friends or quiet ones? What do you like about them?

....

....

....

....

....

5. When you feel down, what kind of partner or group activities can help you feel better?

....

....

....

....

....

6. What is the best gift you have ever received? How about the best gift you have given to someone?

....

....

....

....

....

7. Share a funny story about you and a close friend. It can be recent or something that happened a long time ago.

....

....

....

....

....

Healthy Living

1. List five things you can do to take care of your mental health.

....

....

....

....

....

2. Think about the last time you were under a lot of stress. Describe the situation. Who or what was causing the pressure?

....

....

....

....

....

3. What have you done lately that makes you feel healthy and happy?

....

....

....

....

....

4. What healthy habits do you recall practicing last year?
Are you still practicing them?

....

....

....

....

....

5. If you could spend a day with a person who inspires
you to improve, who would it be and what would you do
together?

....

....

....

....

....

6. How do you remind yourself to make healthier choices when you are coping with fear, sadness, or anxiety?

....

....

....

....

....

7. What negative thoughts might be preventing you from reaching your health-related goals?

....

....

....

....

....

Goals and Purpose

1. What is one adjustment you can make today so that this week goes smoothly?

....

....

....

....

....

2. What are some positive phrases you can say to yourself when things are not going the way you expected them to?

....

....

....

....

....

3. You may have many goals, but as of today, what is your number-one goal?

....

....

....

....

....

4. Where would you like to be two years from now? What do
you see yourself doing?

....

....

....

....

....

5. If you were a mentor to someone who is working toward
a goal, what advice would you give them?

....

....

....

....

....

6. What small things can you add to your routine to make
your mornings or nights more meaningful?

....

....

....

....

....

7. What goal can you set for next week to do something that gives you a sense of purpose?

....

....

....

....

....

Calm and Resiliency

1. When faced with an overwhelming situation, how do you calm yourself so that you can proceed with a clear head?

....

....

....

....

....

2. What are three things or situations you need to say "no" to this week to make your own needs a priority?

....

....

....

....

....

Inspiration exists,
but it must find you working.

—PABLO PICASSO

3. How can you create a calmer environment at home? Describe some specific actions you can take.

....

....

....

....

....

4. What are three types of situations that cause you anxiety? Do you avoid them? What steps can you take to get the anxiety under control in those situations?

....

....

....

....

....

5. If you could take tomorrow afternoon off to do something you enjoy that doesn't cost any money, what would you do?

....

....

....

....

....

6. Write a note to yourself about how proud you are of your ability to bounce back after a setback.

....

....

....

....

....

7. What two tasks or activities did you do this week that made you feel good about yourself?

....

....

....

....

....

Connection and Engagement

1. How can you be more positive and improve your most important relationship—the one you have with yourself?

....

....

....

....

....

2. What social skills can you start practicing this week to more deeply connect with others?

....

....

....

....

....

3. What are some doable ideas you can think of to celebrate the people you love?

....

....

....

....

....

4. Many people need and appreciate help in all different
areas. What kind of assistance can you offer?

....

....

....

....

....

5. What activities do you do with your friends that bring you
true happiness?

....

....

....

....

....

6. Think about the give-and-take in your friendships. What
can you do to become an even better friend?

....

....

....

....

....

7. What self-care activities can you practice alongside
friends or family so that you can all enjoy the benefits
together?

....

....

....

....

....

Healthy Living

1. Do you set boundaries to avoid becoming overwhelmed? Describe some of these boundaries.

....

....

....

....

....

2. Some people might be considered "energy vampires." What can you do to protect yourself from people who are emotionally draining?

....

....

....

....

....

3. At what age did you feel your happiest and healthiest? What did you do then that you do not do now?

....

....

....

....

....

4. Design a nutritious menu. Can you eat this way tomorrow? If not, make a grocery list of the items you will need.

....

....

....

....

....

5. What activities do you do that address your physical, mental, and emotional well-being all in one?

....

....

....

....

....

6. How do you protect yourself from outside negative influences? Describe your strategies.

....

....

....

....

....

7. Do you drink alcohol or use tobacco? What are some alternatives to these substances that you can enjoy instead?

....

....

....

....

....

Goals and Purpose

1. What is your personal definition of purpose in life?

....

....

....

....

....

2. Describe two of the most important events that have happened in your life so far. How have they contributed to your sense of purpose?

....

....

....

....

....

3. What can you plan to do this weekend to accomplish a goal to feel happier?

....

....

....

....

....

4. Which of your recent accomplishments, big or small, have brought you joy?

....

....

....

5. What personal achievement or outcome are you most proud of this week?

....

....

....

....

....

6. Think about everything you want to achieve. What is your number-one short-term goal? Why is that goal important to you?

....

....

....

....

....

7. What steps can you take to accomplish the goal you wrote about yesterday?

....

....

....

....

....

Calm and Resiliency

1. Write about a time when you went somewhere that made you feel so calm that you wished you could stay there all day.

....

....

....

....

....

2. What are three activities you can do to unwind at the end of each day so that you can rest better when you go to sleep?

....

....

....

....

....

No need to hurry. No need to sparkle.
No need to be anyone but yourself.

—VIRGINA WOOLF

3. Share one of your most pleasant dreams and how it made you feel.

....

....

....

....

....

4. Bring to mind the last time you felt happy. Describe what you were doing and any relevant details of the day.

....

....

....

....

....

5. Think back to a recent difficult situation. How did you stay calm or regain your calm later?

....

....

....

....

....

6. List three songs that bring you a sense of serenity when
you listen to them.

....

....

....

....

....

7. How quickly do you bounce back after adversity? What
event or situation helped you become more resilient?

....

....

....

....

....

Connection and Engagement

1. What can you do to improve your relationship with someone you love?

....

....

....

....

....

2. Who do you need to forgive? What are some ways you can go about it?

....

....

....

....

....

3. Resentment is lingering bitterness. If you feel resentful toward someone, how might you let it go? Sometimes it is a matter of creating boundaries.

....

....

....

....

....

4. Who do you most admire? What qualities does this person (or people) have?

....

....

....

....

....

5. List three people you are most grateful for in your life. What have they done to make you feel this way?

....

....

....

....

....

6. What are a few things you can do to show your appreciation to the people you identified yesterday?

....

....

....

....

....

7. Is there a cause that is important to you? How can you offer your support?

....

....

....

....

....

Healthy Living

1. List five items on your to-do list that are causing you stress. How will you cope with each?

....

....

....

....

....

2. What are your views on mental health?

....

....

....

....

....

3. Check in with yourself. How is your mental health today?

....

....

....

....

....

4. If you could talk to a therapist about your mental health, what would you share?

....

....

....

....

....

5. If a loved one asked you what you thought about counseling, how would you respond?

....

....

....

....

....

6. Describe the emotions you are feeling today. Are any more prominent than the others?

....

....

....

....

....

7. Write a note to yourself about how much you care about your emotional health and why it is important to nurture it.

....

....

....

....

....

Goals and Purpose

1. How is your life different today compared to three years ago? What might have caused the differences?

....

....

....

....

....

2. What inspirational or motivational quote do you identify with the most? Why?

....

....

....

....

....

3. How do you feel if you hit obstacles when working toward your goals?

....

....

....

....

....

4. What is the biggest lesson you learned in the past year about yourself as far as what is important to you?

....

....

....

5. Do you have a book on your must-read list? How about a must-see movie? What about the book or movie makes you want to experience it?

....

....

....

....

....

6. The weekend may be the perfect time to accomplish something you have been meaning to do. What would you like to accomplish this weekend? How will you do it?

....

....

....

....

....

7. If you had extra time to volunteer for an organization, charity, or community drive, what type of service would you find most rewarding? Why?

....

....

....

....

....

Calm and Resiliency

1. Identify a negative thought you want to let go of. What are some steps you can take to let it go?

....

....

....

....

....

2. Write about a time when you felt anxious. What were you experiencing physically and emotionally? What might you do differently if you were in that situation now?

....

....

....

....

....

No one should be discouraged who can make constant progress, even though it be slow.

—PLATO

3. If you shared your negative thoughts or anxious feelings with a loved one, what would they likely tell you?

....

....

....

....

....

4. Breathing exercises are an excellent way to help you feel calm. How often do you practice them? Describe how you feel before and after a deep breath.

....

....

....

....

....

5. What are your greatest fears? What steps have you taken to try to let them go?

....

....

....

....

....

6. Are your fears realistic? List any hard evidence you have to support them.

....

....

....

....

....

7. Breathing exercises, mindfulness, and meditation can all reduce anxiety levels. What other anxiety-reducing tools or ideas have you heard of or practiced?

....

....

....

....

....

Connection and Engagement

1. List five things you can do to improve your relationship with your loved ones.

....

....

....

....

....

2. What boundaries do you need to set with people who make you feel drained?

....

....

....

....

....

3. Do you say "no" to people who tend to guilt you into doing things you do not want to do? Why or why not?

....

....

....

....

....

4. What can you do to make others feel happier when they spend time with you?

....

....

....

....

....

5. If you need to have a difficult conversation and thinking about it is making you anxious, what steps can you take to reduce your anxiety?

....

....

....

....

....

6. Think about a movie or TV show where the main character says and does things you wish you could do. How can you be more like that person?

....

....

....

....

....

7. List five activities you can do with your friends or family in the coming weeks.

....

....

....

....

....

Healthy Living

1. What were three of the main obstacles to living a healthier life you encountered this past year?

....

....

....

....

....

2. How did you overcome the obstacles you wrote about yesterday?

....

....

....

....

....

3. Describe your mental and emotional health today in as much detail as possible.

....

....

....

....

....

4. What will you do to continue taking care of your health next year?

....

....

....

....

....

5. How has journaling helped you live a happier life?

....

....

....

....

....

6. What physical activities would you like to introduce into your life? Why did you choose those activities?

....

....

....

....

....

7. What can you do to prevent stress from affecting you in the future?

....

....

....

....

....

....

Goals and Purpose

1. Think about your most recent accomplishments. Write a note telling yourself why you feel proud for achieving them.

....

....

....

....

....

2. If you could achieve anything next year, what would it be?

....

....

....

....

....

3. How will you start preparing to reach your short-term goals?

....

....

....

....

....

4. Think back to when you started this journal and compare how you felt then to how you feel now. What are the main differences?

....

....

....

....

....

5. Write five positive affirmations you can use when you finish this journal to use every day to feel good.

....

....

....

....

....

6. Take a deep breath and reflect on everything you have accomplished since you started this journal. List the top five.

....

....

....

....

....

7. Write a note congratulating yourself for completing
52 weeks of journaling. You did it! Be proud.

....

....

....

....

....

You have power over your
mind—not outside events.
Realize this, and you will find strength.

—MARCUS AURELIUS

RESOURCES

APP

Calm.com: An app for finding calm and peacefulness

AUDIOBOOK

Brené Brown. *The Power of Vulnerability: Teachings on Authenticity, Connection and Courage.* Louisville, CO: Sounds True, 2012.

WEBSITES

CrisisTextLine.org: 24/7 crisis counseling via text message

HealthUnlocked.com: The world's largest social network for health

Talkspace.com: Online therapy with a licensed therapist

TherapistAid.com/therapy-worksheets: Free mental health handouts and worksheets

TheTrevorProject.org: Crisis intervention for the LGBTQ+ community

Turn2me.ie: Free support groups

REFERENCES

Aristotle. "Ethica Nicomachea (Nicomachean Ethics)," in *The Basic Works of Aristotle*. Edited by Richard McKeon. New York: Random House, 1941.

Aurelius, Marcus. *Meditations: A New Translation*. Translated by Gregory Hays. New York: Random House, 2003.

Brown, Brené. *Daring Greatly*. New York: Avery Books, 2015.

Dalí, Salvador. *Diary of a Genius*. Translated by Richard Howard. London: Creation Books, 1998.

de Saint-Exupéry, Antoine. *The Little Prince*. Translated by Irene Testot-Ferry. Hertfordshire, UK: Wordsworth Editions Limited, 1995.

Elliot, Jeffrey M. *Conversations with Maya Angelou*. Jackson, MS: University Press of Mississippi, 1989.

France, Anatole. *The Crime of Sylvestre Bonnard*. United States: Library of Alexandria, 2020.

Geldard, Richard G. *Remembering Heraclitus*. Herndon Farms, VA: Lindisfarne Books, 2000.

Hadot, Pierre. *What Is Ancient Philosophy?* Translated by Michael Chase. Cambridge, MA: The Belknap Press of Harvard University Press, 2002.

Matisse, Henri. *Jazz*. Translated by Sophie Hawkes. New York: George Braziller, 1992.

MichBusiness. "MichBusiness Wellness & Wellbeing Resources Guide." Accessed April 5, 2021. michbusiness.com/wp-content/uploads/2021/03/WellnessResourceGuideMB.pdf.

"Modern Living: Ozmosis in Central Park." *TIME*, October 4, 1976. content.time.com/time/subscriber/article/0,33009,918412,00.html.

Novotney, Amy. "The Risks of Social Isolation: Psychologists Are Studying How to Combat Loneliness in Those Most at Risk, Such as Older Adults." *Monitor on Psychology* 50, no. 5 (May 2019): 32. apa.org/monitor/2019/05/ce-corner-isolation.

Plato. "Sophist 261b.," in *Plato in Twelve Volumes*, volume 12. Translated by Harold N. Fowler. Cambridge, MA: Harvard University Press, 1921. perseus.tufts.edu/hopper/text?doc=Perseus%3Atext%3A1999.01.0172%3Atext%3DSoph.%3Asection%3D261b.

Van Gogh, Vincent. *The Letters of Vincent van Gogh*. Translated by Ronald de Leeuw. Edited by Mark W. Roskill. New York: Penguin Books, 2003.

Villasante, Tomás R. *Las Ciudades Hablan*. Editorial Nueva Sociedad: Buenos Aires, 1994.

Woolf, Virginia. *A Room of One's Own*. London: Renard Press, 2020.

ACKNOWLEDGMENTS

I want to thank Jed and Carol for their guidance and patience and the rest of my publishing team for their willingness to work with me. Thanks to my husband, Clarence, for his time and for being nearby during this journey. And to Chase, just for being.

ABOUT THE AUTHOR

Cynthia Catchings, LCSW-S, LCSW-C, MSSW is a psychotherapist and clinical social worker in private practice, an adjunct professor at the University of Texas Rio Grande Valley, and a mental health consultant. Her vast experiences include working as a case management supervisor, a psychotherapist, and a Supervisor II for the Texas Department of Family and Protective Services. Catchings is the former executive director of a family violence shelter. Now executive director of the Women's Emotional Wellness Center with offices in Texas and Virginia, she is committed to ensuring that every person learns how to practice self-care to minimize and eventually eradicate the emotional problems that affect us. She also has taught French, Spanish, and English as a second language for more than 15 years and has traveled globally to conduct mental health ethnographic research in more than 30 countries.